ANALYTICS IN TEACHING & LEARNING

DR DHEERAJ MEHROTRA

Contents

Preface

Analytics in teaching & learning is an idea toward making learning a priority. Open communication is a foundation for creating an academic atmosphere and cultivating innovation. The students' thoughts on research can be significantly expanded. The ability to reveal scientific achievements can be enhanced considerably by exchanging ideas through classroom teaching and learning styles.

The book Analytics in Teaching & Learning is one such initiative to review and share the teaching styles and modalities for the needful.

Happy Learning, Guys!

www.authordheerajmehrotra.com

ONE

Analytics in Teaching

We know that learning does not stop when our students leave the lecture theatre. Studying at the schools and colleges should be an enriching experience that takes in all aspects of life, social and cultural and educational—exhibit higher degrees of awareness, acceptance of cultural diversity and an increase in their cultural capital. Students also experience other teaching preferences; they can master the local teaching and learning skills, develop their self-confidence, and help prepare themselves for higher academics. The objective has to be to harness the learning potentials in particular. My Vision with teaching and learning goes with the spectrum of Catering to the stakeholders via these schools; we aim to set up a culture of learning which shall prove to be world-class through the mission and vision set by the

society. I am eyeing the directives and the passion of the schools' vision and the mission of the workforce, and the priorities towards making education of International standards and development of curriculum at par with CBSE and other Boards.

The dedication and expertise shall empower the existing schools and set up quality benchmarks through various parameters and cross-checks with mentoring and training of teachers as a priority through the adoption of technology/ LMS/ Blended Learning/ BYOD culture and exploring the expectations by the various boards and the requisites of the local authorities as well as the national boards. The implementation of the parameters mentioned above in the chain of our schools shall also cater to setting up our standards with the march of time with policies and framework and a daily reporting system which would include the attendance/ implementation via the ERP system of cloud-based connectivity. I am also looking forward to setting up this quality benchmark through my cloud connection with the best professionals in the country and abroad for exchange visits and training sessions for various inceptions and ideas to explore the density and quality learning derivatives as a priority.

The teachers need to aim to work for the knowledge centre to explore the novel approaches to teaching and learning various practices like experiential learning, STEAM, Art Integration, Design Thinking, competency-based education, development of social and emotional skills, life skills, quality circles, kaizen, digital body language, online reputation management, digital quotient and attaining goals promote the rooted Indian ethos among the students at large with the exploration of the new age parenting expectations. I am sure this shall set up an excellent benchmark for others to emulate through the model of feedback and QUALITY IMPROVEMENT PLAN for the Schools in particular.

There has to be an analytical preview system, emphasising a feasibility report with the school principals afterwards with a proposal to deliver an improved model on the go with the recommendations. The peer review shall be conducted under the set parameters of Quality Guidelines for schools and shall be followed by the offerings to the schools as a frequent quality check. The objective shall be to promote excellence with a global dimension that is central to children's education to face the challenges of the 21st century with courage, confidence, and strength of character. The teachers and the heads of schools need to aim to cover and conduct peer reviews of all our schools in the first five months to work on the expansion and promotion of the brand. The peer review of the schools may be the process as per the guidelines of the Schools Quality Assessment and Accreditation, CBSE/ NABET/ QCI International, USA/ Quality Council of India.

The classroom as a feature to taste the teacher's expertise lies in momentum with the engagement of the wards in particular.

ENGAGE ME OR ENRAGE ME; the Choice is yours.

Ma'am, please tell us something new! This is already in the book. Comes the reply to any subject related interactions today in today's classrooms. To the surprise of many, the Walls and Friend Requests have come across as more popular than HELLO or Hi!

Are we on the same page? The choice is ours to intercept the juncture regarding making the best of job operations, delivering the best with pride and honour and above all, meeting standards the requisite for the schools to flourish. The marketing mantras sponsor the best the teachers' satisfaction but in a new role of cyber presence now. The need for today towards the teaching segment has dwelled with intelligence and IT-friendly requisites by all. Quality Education is reflected by the involvement of the Quality Infrastructure in the learning arena, which otherwise is not of any use and Children Friendly. The parents are requested to make their choices today for admission in the majority of the mushrooming shops around the country more like any other service industry with the option to have around the school, the classes and even they are told to leave their wards in the class as a trial run for them to decide of taste. Computers, software, CDs and Smart Toys ought to be considered as a supplement to the other, more concrete learning activities like completing puzzles, building with Lego and blocks, reading books, creating art projects and playing on the playground...", is evident by our observations and research, out of the present-day scenario. On very grounds of improvement planning and the paradigm shift with education being characterised by technology-enabled instructions, collaborative learning, multidisciplinary problem-solving and promoting critical thinking skills, e-learning, a household name for the students today, offers a wide variety of ICT enabled classroom solutions for learning the Smart Way! It allows a user-friendly option for learners to integrate what is desired and acquired to their requirements class and level.

No talking boys and girls can no longer be the most common vocabulary for the teachers for the new learner demands and explore the power of engagement within the classrooms and that of the narration to examine the connection via the cyber world with the teachers in reality. Put Your Camera ON! Turn your Video On! is the new normal!

No wonder you tell a child to write an essay as homework; they are bound to download the content to present before you the next day, making you baffled by the interest of the many others lying in the queue. The parents often think of this as a menace out of the challenging work wisdom they possess to earn their daily living. Their frames are not yet over with more demands for the CD-Burner and Scanner for more computing and smart-study, as they call it. The only option available to the poor parents of the IT age is to ponder over for solace and accept novel ways to convince their future generations regarding motivations and guided involvement.

The TEACHERS need to harness the requirements to the best of their abilities and interest further. They need to be dependent on some SMART teaching options available to them in the classroom to make the learning scenario enjoyable to the kids. This offers an innovative methodology to educate every child of the country with specialisation in the art of scalability involving people, processes, and technology—the focus applicants to build innovative capabilities and performance at the institutional level continuously.

We have DIGITALLY ORIENTED CLASSROOMS now in every school, but does that solve the purpose? I doubt my experience. It is the mindset of the teachers, the educators, which needs to function well. The Teacher ought to be a TRAINER/ LEARNER/ ALL ROUNDER, with their presence in the CYBERSPACE mandatory. No longer having an EMAIL ID and expertise of MS OFFICE but more and more...viz....having a WEBSITE, BLOG, WiKi, and more, apart from being SOCIALLY NETWORKED 24x7. Also, w,e need to remember that Teachers become enamoured with YouTube, TED, and WatchKnowLearn or any Ready Reckoner Web Content of interest with Quality and Cream!

As teachers, we must not use technology as a silicon coating but harness the power of technology to connect with our students. No more, it is about copying and pasting what we have been doing over the years. Power corrupts politicians, so PowerPoint corrupts the teachers if it has just slides and no explanations. For a matter of thought and intelligence, the platform should be shared for show rather than expecting it to be the only parcel for knowledge delivery. There is a specific need to implement a new way of teaching through technology, and hence a digital pedagogy is required the most. The teachers need to introspect how children may learn in this networked environment. We can't simply take a textbook and deliver it digitally; somewhat, the need here is to explore the power to harness the best via connectivity and creativity to connect.

We can't think and re-discover the chalkboard and make it a smartboard to deliver knowledge. What is required is a novel mindset of love, care and delivery of priorities for our children within classrooms. We ultimately need a different paradigm for teaching, a different pedagogy that talks about creation, control of chaos, connection to correcting, and consumption to creation. The teachers need to change their thinking about how they will use technology in education.

For sure, we live in a world of change, There are great tweets each minute, and great Facebook page views each minute. The academic Donald Norman describes skeuomorphism in terms of cultural constraints: interactions with a system learned only through culture. The period intensifies the tech world with pride. The world has only been used in the tech industry for a few years, where its meaning has changed, says Dan O'Hara, an academic at Birmingham City University. "Skeumorphs are not strictly something that can be designed," he says. "They occur unintentionally when aesthetic styles are inherited without thinking." The photo views of Flickr, which mounts to n' undefined, explore the universal learning of repute. Each minute of over 47,000 app downloads on the apple store encapsulates a new phase of dimensional learning taking place out of the hunger for knowledge. Of course, all these facts did not exist before 2004. The availability of data online fascinates the new learner in multiple ways who tend to be a multitasker in pave to grab the unknown. To sound far-fetched but true, the schools over the years have not changed. They have taken the same task to be limited to rows and columns with a teacher at pace. They, typically at large, have no technology; hence there has been no change. There are reports, too, "Failed iPad Experiment Shows BYOD Belongs in Schools.", "LA. Cancels iPads-in-the-schools program: a failure of vision, not technology. Despite all our heavy investments in schools, there is a failure in our strategy or the idea to implement the best technology in education. And above all, it appears to be the inability of our pedagogy. One of our mistakes as educators is CTRL + C & CTRL + V. Necessarily as COPY and PASTE for this just can't solve the concerns but expands the issue in particular. This is one of the mistakes we get to govern while implementing technology in our schools.

Similarly, the conclusion fetches the scenario of apparent reasons for shifting the teaching into a new realm. The core teaching principles having a shift need an activated model to conclude without looking back in perfection. The teachers need to be an advocate for holistic education. This transforms the learners in a big way to assist learning and make it happen within the classrooms. Teachers need to keep things simple and do what works for them. For us, the teachers cannot teach the way we were taught. Above all, the students, at large, would only like the subject if they like the teacher, and this is one of the solitaire truths for any holy classroom in particular. Teachers need to have a wellness routine planning sheet, getting the win-win approach of the happiness index of the students, roll number wise. Indeed, classroom management has been identified as a primary concern for teachers, and if they don't get along with the learners as bosses or clients with affection, the management of the class appears slang. The teachers in the majority have a wrong notion that classroom management is much to do with discipline only and is limited to the children being quiet in the class.

In contrast, the goals include identifying misconceptions about managing the teaching, the students and the consequences. The teachers of age need to broaden the very conception of classroom management and ultimately provide a framework among their colleagues for developing their classroom management plan. Engaging the children in instructions often leads to classroom management but is limited to a classic time only. For having an activated classroom, there has to be a thoughtful physical environment supported by establishing caring relationships and implementing engaging instructions.

Some of the Teaching Strategies with WOW traits within classrooms feature as follows:

1. Lecturing

For sure, Lecturing can mean an instructional talk, or it can take the form of a stern, one-sided conversation. It is in part through engaging students in interaction, using questions and answers, that some of the limitations of lectures can be overcome. The course has to be Lively, Educative, Creative, Thought-provoking, Understanding, Relevant and Enjoyable.

2. Circle Time Activities

A Circle time, also called group time, refers to a group of people sitting together for an activity involving everyone. Circle time is usually light and fun and aims to get children ready for learning. Consider the three essential questions of Why, What, and How. This can go well both for the teachers and the students in particular.

3. Simulation Method

Activating classrooms via Simulations refers to instructional scenarios where the learner is placed in a "world" defined by the teacher. They represent a reality within which students interact. The teacher controls the parameters of this "Engagement" and uses it to achieve the desired instructional results.

4. Modelling Method

Modelling during teaching is an instructional strategy in which the teacher demonstrates a new concept or approach to learning, and students learn by observing. Whenever a teacher explains an idea to a student, that teacher is modelling. It activates engagement in an absolute sense.

5. Online Learning Tools

These are the Most Popular Digital Education Tools For Teachers And Learners. The most common ones include Edmodo, an educational tool that connects teachers and students and assimilates into a social network. Google Classrooms and Kahoot are other commonly used platforms.

6. Game Simulation

As one of the innovative ways of teaching, the use of simulation games implies that the teacher values the unique needs of individual students. Learning is an active process rather than a passive one during this process. It encapsulates the importance of students' examining their values and the values of others in particular.

7. Collaborative Problem Solving

Very collaborative problem-solving acts as "the capacity of an individual to effectively engage in a process whereby two or more agents attempt to solve a problem by sharing the understanding and effort required to come to a solution and pooling their knowledge and skills in totality. It activates learning by doing hands-on.

8. Discussion Groups

The Discussion method of teaching is a group activity which involves the teacher and the student in defining the problem and deriving its solution. It is a constructive process that consists of listening, thinking, and deriving conversation skills on priority.

9. Peer Instruction

Peer teaching involves one or more students teaching other students in a particular subject area and builds on the belief that "to teach is to learn twice" (Whitman, 1998)." For students, peer learning can lead to improved attitudes and a more personalised, engaging, and collaborative learning experience, leading to higher achievement. The experience can deepen their understanding of the subject and impart confidence to peer teachers.

10. Active Learning

Active learning is an approach to instruction that involves actively engaging students with the course material through discussions, problem-solving, case studies, role plays and other methods. The process is towards giving students a time limit to complete the task. The strategy identifies to Stop the activity and debrief. Call on a few students or groups of students to share their thoughts and tie them into the next steps of your lecture.

11. Project-Based Learning

Project-Based Learning is a teaching method in which students gain knowledge and skills by working for an extended period to investigate and respond to an authentic, engaging, and complex question, problem, or challenge. Project-based teachers ensure that students understand the learning goals and why they matter towards catching them young and innocent.

12. Unit Tests

Unit tests are conducted in the school to evaluate the summative assessment of the teaching-learning process. The main aim of the unit test is to isolate each unit of the system to identify, analyse and fix the defects. The test is different from assessment and evaluation in the following manner towards excellence.

13. Assignments

The Assignment method is the most common teaching method in schools, particularly in teaching Science. It is a technique usually used in the teaching and learning process. It is an instructional technique that comprises guided information, self-learning, writing skills, and report preparation. It also includes simple homework assignments as one of the standard learning and evaluation methods.

14. Classroom Quizzing and Brain Gym:

Ask questions and make their brain work brighter. Example: Ask them to make the number 9 using their thumb altogether. Ask them to write their first name in ENGLISH using their index finger in the air.

15. Remedial Teaching

Identify weak students and engage them through peer learning. Involve them through partners such as 12.00 O Clock Partner or other time frames. This can even happen before assembly or after school.

16. Presentations

Engage them through the presentation skills via Technology. Some widely used presentation platforms include PREZI, MS Powerpoint and KEYNOTE.

17. Zoom In

Let the students observe gradual portions of an image and ask them to write and engage in writing. Ask them what new things they see. How does it change their thinking? Repeat the reveal and questioning until the whole image is revealed.

18. Chalk Talk

Using the Chalk Talk Strategy to engage them via homework analysis. The chalk talk method is an excellent way to ignite shy students. It engages the learners, promotes independent thinking and allows them to have an equal say. Here the teacher tells the students to analyse their thought analysis. The students rotate as a team via different prompts. The output is shared in public.

19. Work Books & Step Inside Routine

It gives the option to students to answer questions using Step Inside virtually. You let them step inside the character of the individuals. It is like stepping inside the situation in particular. Suitable for English, History, and exploring historical events from a specific perspective. Example Thinking or wondering about a soldier's perspective.

20. Posters and Reading Conference

Showcase the Posters and ask the children to read and interact. This goes via interactions randomly with peers and teachers. It integrates Visual Literacy like I see I wonder. The use of posters and the opportunity to read the content individually or as per the lucky system works wonders.

21. Self-Learning Tools

This is a live example of using learning tools as a practical approach. Some online tools include Google Digital Garage, LinkedIn Learning, Coursera, Khan Academy, edX and Academic Earth.

22. Competitions

This includes the various formats like Debates/ Interactions/ Recitation/ Writing/ Fashion Shows/ Speech Contest/ Case Study Presentations.

23. Object-Based Learning

Object-based learning is a form of active learning. A student-centred learning approach uses objects to create a more profound learning experience. It is an educational method that actively uses authentic or replica material things. These objects can include artworks, artefacts, archival materials, or digital representations of unique items.

24. Class Summary

The Class Summary integrates classroom learning via engagement as a priority. To make it effective, the students must first practice the imparted skills of identifying and describing the main topic or activity in a class and giving some coherent, sequenced details. The idea is to catch them young and innocent towards learning as the ultimate.

25. Club Activities

This leads to bodily awareness, independent thinking, problem-solving and reasoning, positive self-image, talent management and collaboration & teamwork. The other activities include co-curricular activities such as public speaking, debate and dramatics, creative writing, eco-club, quizzing, astronomy, dance, photography, philately, trekking, film appreciation and even cooking.

26. Adaptive Teaching

Adaptive teaching as an educational method aims to achieve a common instructional goal with learners whose individual differences, such as prior achievement, aptitude, or learning styles, differ. It assists in providing a personalised education, aiming at providing efficient, effective, and customised learning paths to the learners. It also helps the teachers to engage each student. It is a student data-driven approach to adjusting the direction and pace of learning, enabling the delivery of personalised learning at scale in totality.

27. Cross Over Learning

The concept of crossover learning refers to a comprehensive understanding of learning that bridges formal and informal learning settings toward teaching excellence. It is one of the techniques used to provide personalised learning and aims to deliver efficient, effective, and customised learning paths to engage each student.

28. Case Study

The case study methodology incorporates learning by engaging the students in discussing scenarios that represent real-world examples, such as Distractions Within Classrooms. This method is learner-centred, with intense interaction between participants, such as brainstorming. This further makes them develop skills, build their knowledge and work together as a group to examine the case.

29. Self-Learning

Using Google Earth Educational Tools. This helps visualise the abstract concepts across a global canvas, allowing students to connect what they learn inside to what they experience in their daily lives, community, and to the larger world. Google Earth's creation tools allow you to create your parts.

30. Team Projects

This may include creating a poster, Making a PowerPoint presentation, Designing a model, Making a shoebox diorama, Using a 3-panel display board, Making a timeline, creating a board game incorporating key elements, and writing a poem, among others.

31. Research Projects

Research-based teaching means that students conduct research independently and with an open outcome in their courses. This teaching and learning methodology focuses on the joint acquisition of new skills by lecturers and students. This requires the teachers to reflect on their role as teachers and learners.

32. Gesturing

This form of teaching integrates the learner's gestures, allowing indexing of conceptual instability moments. The teachers, during this process, make use of those gestures to gain access to a student's thinking. The learners discover novel ideas from the gestures produced during a lesson during the process.

33. Instructional Videos

This is a prevalent methodology to integrate the showcase of learning using videos. The instructions electronically in videos guide the students to follow a specific path, and learning is depicted during the process.

34. Social Media

The ultimate use of social media in teaching assists the students with the ability to get more helpful information. It makes them connected with learning groups and other educational platforms online. It allows the students to share their queries, concerns and comments, making education convenient. These tools allow the students and institutions to explore multiple opportunities to improve learning methods.

35. Humour

Humour in the classroom explores the inception of Teaching styles that have changed significantly over the years. It allows the switch from the traditional way education was delivered through recitation and memorisation techniques. In contrast, the modern way of doing things involves interactive methods with humour as a priority now for sure with the march of time and tide as a reality in practice for schools and teachers need to dwell as a hobby for now. The inception is eyed and segmented towards the participative nature of students within classrooms to get the connection and make learning a priority for both the teacher and the learner in momentum to share the cause of learning, making the best for all.

36. Panel Discussion

During this teaching process, the process is initiated through observation and listening. In a Panel Discussion, a designated or an invited group of students act as a panel, and the remaining class members act as the audience. The committee further discusses the selected questions and topics in particular. A panel leader is chosen, and they summarise the panel discussion and opens the conversation to the audience. A question and answer session follows the process for clarity and collaboration.

37. Modelling

Modelling is an instructional strategy in which the teacher demonstrates a new concept or an approach to make learning a priority with the preface of teaching excellence and WOW spectrum towards the taste and requirements of the learners. The students during this phase enjoy the learning through observation. The teaching is done by observing. Whenever a teacher demonstrates a concept for a student, that teacher is modelling as a measure.

38. Discovery Method

The Discovery Learning Method is mandated through the "Guided Discovery" format, which refers to a teaching and learning environment where students actively discover knowledge by exploring options through working and exploring ideas. It is a constructivist theory based on the idea that students construct their understanding and knowledge of the world through experiencing things and reflecting on those experiences. It is assisted through inquiry-based instruction and is considered a constructivist-based education approach.

39. Demonstration Method

As the word says, demonstration, the module covers showcasing with explanation in particular. It is used to communicate an idea with the assistance of visuals like flip charts, posters, PowerPoint, and other online or offline tools. A demonstration teaches someone how to make or do something in a step-by-step process. It is suitable for science subjects.

40. Role Playing Method

Role-play is a technique that allows students to explore realistic situations by interacting with other people in an organised manner towards developing real-life skills and experiencing an environment of choice and chance. It provides an additional learning delight for the students, and they can very well understand the scenario being discussed during the process.

41. Oral Questions

This methodology allows the teacher to engage the students via assignments orally. It initiates and involves the teacher, where probing is conducted among the students. Here the questions are floated to think about what they know regarding a topic, and in a verbal format, they respond. The Questions typically allow the teacher to keep a point of the discussion focused on the intended objective and the learning objective through the involvement of all the students at length.

42. Questioning Method

This is an add on method to the Oral Questions and may include the written assignments. The objective is to engage the students via connections and tasks.

43. Discussion Method

Here we follow the collaborative exchange of ideas among the students to ignite students thinking, learning, problem-solving, understanding and decision-making abilities.

44. Problem Based Learning

This identifies the engagement of the kids through Question or Assignment based learning. The teacher takes the problem/ assignment and works on it with the students and significant contributors. This acts as one of the easy-going tools for examining them during revision modules.

45. Assignments

This includes work assignments, routine jobs, class tests, homework and online reflections.

46. Make free and open source technologies available to teachers and students

The objective is towards specific connections via the directions from the UNESCO, Open educational resources and open access digital tools must be supported. Education cannot thrive with ready-made content built outside of the pedagogical space and outside of human relationships between teachers and students.

Nor can education be dependent on digital platforms controlled by private companies.

47. Cross Over Learning

The crossover learning format entirely refers to a comprehensive understanding of learning that bridges a classroom's formal and informal learning settings. Experiences from everyday life can enrich the learning through this medium; informal learning can be deepened by adding questions and knowledge from the school. This format aims to combine the strengths of formal and informal learning environments and seeks to provide students with the best of both. As per boardteachers.com, an effective method for crossover learning involves teachers proposing a question or problem in the classroom to be solved during museum visits or field trips. Children can learn by collecting photos, taking down notes, or asking other people for their thoughts. They then present what they learned back in the classroom to illuminate the given problem further.

48. Dramatic Method

It is more like drama in teaching or dramatics in education. This, at random, allows students to explore the curriculum using several of Gardner's multiple intelligences. Here the kids are fully involved in learning with drama as a practice. They are inect through the activities and do role plays of characters on the subject of learning. The process activates at length, developing their skills and, particularly, their bodies, minds, and emotions, yielding creativity and innovation as a common practice.

49. Pen Pals

A coined word of yesteryears has an interpreted meaning today. Teachers and educators worldwide share their experience with global project-based learning through PenPal platforms. One of the schools practising this says: We set the children up with their email addresses and put these under one central email alias. This allowed the teachers to screen each email exchange to ensure it was appropriate and then prepare spelling lists and topic word banks based on the sales. We moved to weekly deals because the messages were now arriving within seconds of hitting "send," we moved to weekly deals. This allowed our students to breeze through the usual "getting to know you" questions and move on to topics that allowed for meaningful cultural interactions.

50. Audio Tutorial Lessons

Also known as PODCASTING in a novel sense, the format is widely used in schools. The audio-tutorial instruction is the most complete and most well-documented method of auditory presentation among teachers.

51. Mobile Applications

Mobile apps help in systematic learning in a big way. The best part is that Mobile learning (m-learning) is education via the Internet with the help of personal mobile devices. This is encompassed with BYOD- Bring Your Device format in schools where devices like tablets and smartphones assist learning to a better level. It helps obtain learning materials through mobile apps, social interactions and online educational hubs.

52. Flowcharts

This is a diagrammatic way of teaching where each activity is represented through a symbol. These are joined through the direction arrows and are connected through lines.

53. Brain Storming

This is an act of idea generation. This activity encourages students to focus on a topic and contribute to the free flow of ideas. Ideally, it is initiated by the teacher as a facilitator who may begin a brainstorming session by posing a question or a problem or by introducing a topic. Students then, in the process, express possible answers, relevant words, and ideas.

54. Simulation Games

The use of simulation games within classrooms implies that the teacher values the unique needs of individual students. It signifies that learning is an active process and hence has to equip with innovation and creativity.

55. Psychomotor Development Methods

Psychomotor learning is demonstrated by physical skills such as movement, coordination, and manipulation of learning traits among students. It delivers organised patterns of muscular activities guided by signals from the environment.

56. Inquiry Method

Inquiry-based learning is an approach that encapsulates the student's role in the learning process. Rather than the teacher telling students what they need to know, students are encouraged to explore the material, ask questions, and share ideas.

57. Ensure scientific literacy within the curriculum.

As guided and reflected by UNESCO, this is the right time for deep reflection on curriculum, particularly as we struggle against the denial of scientific knowledge and actively fight misinformation. Teachers can help and guide students using various topics via scientific literacy.

58. Webinars

A webinar is an interface over the Internet. A much talked about and explored during the CORONA times globally. The webinar allows interaction between the students and the professors online. When used in a classroom as a medium of teaching, it helps remove the scepticism from the minds of the shy students to raise their hands and ask questions in a classroom full of students—a very effective tool in particular.

59. Process Approach Method

The process approach is a method of thinking applied to understand and plan the sequence and interactions of processes in the system. Teaching here is integrated through a process and the interactions of these processes as part of the teaching and learning system in a classroom scenario.

60. Hands-On

Hands-on learning is a teaching pattern of imparting education in which children learn by doing themselves. Instead of simply listening to a teacher on the specified subject, the student engages with the subject matter to solve a problem or create something via hands-on experience via engagement and teamwork.

61. Seminars

A seminar is an opportunity to learn or explore learning via interactions. Particularly in academics, a meeting may have several purposes, such as a lecture, where the participants engage in the discussion of an academic subject to gain a better insight into the matter. For a typical classroom scenario, it works as an option for learning with pleasure.

62. Chalk and Talk

A Chalk Talk is a much preferred and silent activity that allows all students to reflect on what they know and then share their thinking and wonderings while connecting to their classmates' thoughts. "Chalk & Talk" is a formal teaching method with a blackboard and the teacher's voice as its focal point. This method is used in classrooms across the world. Despite the name, there is no chalk involved with the advent of technology, only paper and pencils, markers, or digital devices.

63. Laboratory

The School labs are an excellent place for students, which help them enhance their learning by understanding the theoretical concepts of science taught in classrooms. The set-up of the student-friendly has to be encapsulated. Well-designed laboratories make science experiments fun and help students achieve good academic results. It salutes the framework of learning through demonstrations and hands-on learning.

64. Content Analysis

Content analysis is a research method that allows the qualitative data collected in research to be analysed systematically and reliably so that generalisations can be made about the categories of interest to the researcher. It is one of the ACTIVE RESEARCH activities by educators, and the research findings help deliver learning as a priority for schools.

65. Reciprocal Teaching

Reciprocal teaching is an instructional activity where students become the teacher in small group reading sessions. Common teaching refers to a classroom activity where students are shown strategies to understand a reading better. As one of the periodic models of education, RT helps students learn to guide group discussions using four techniques: summarising, question generating, clarifying, and predicting in particular.

66. Assignment Method

With the help of the Assignment Method, evaluation based learning is possible. Using this process of assignment method, the teacher delivers an assignment with clear instructions, milestones, objectives and grading criteria based on an outcome that students need to achieve as an activity scheduled over a phase of time. The teacher accordingly monitors and further delivers the feedback to students as they solve the assignment and share the input towards improvement.

67. Micro Teaching

It is a part of teacher training, but it helps students learn a lot. Microteaching can also define as a teaching technique mainly used in teachers' pre-service education to train them systematically by allowing them to experiment with main teacher behaviours in the real-life scenario. It more or less helps as a revision module on the go, which enables teacher trainees to practice a skill by teaching a short lesson to a small number of pupils. Usually, a micro class of 5 to 10 minutes is taught to four or five fellow students.

68. Mastery Learning

Mastery learning, also known as competency-based teaching, is a set of group-based, individualised teaching and learning strategies based on the preface that students will achieve a high level of understanding in a given domain if given enough time. It ensures that the students obtain mastery of a given topic before moving on to the next unit. The objective is to gain high achievement levels through active instruction, time, and perseverance.

69. Direct Instructions

Direct instruction is a teacher-directed teaching method. This means that the teacher stands in front of a classroom and presents the information. The teachers give explicit, guided instructions to the students. To make it simple and effective, direct instruction refers to instructional approaches that are structured, sequenced, and led by teachers, and the presentation of academic content to students by teachers, such as in a lecture or demonstration within the classrooms over a specified interval.

70. Flipped Classrooms

A flipped classroom is a pattern of mixed learning where students are introduced to content at home and practice working through it at school. It adheres to the reverse of the more common practice of the traditional format of presenting new content at school and then assigning homework to the students. In Colorado, two high school teachers named Jonathan Bergmann and Aaron Sams pioneered it.

71. Kinaesthetic Learning

Kinaesthetic-tactile techniques are combined with visual and auditory study techniques, producing multi-sensory learning. These activities help enrich learning into long-term memory by turning a lesson into a physical experience for the students. Kinaesthetic learning happens when we have a hands-on experience. An example of a kinaesthetic learning experience is when a child learns to use a swing or ride a bike. The students in the process can read instructions or even look forward to listening to instructions. Still, deep learning occurs via the process of doing as a hands-on learning approach in particular.

72. Differentiated Instruction

Differentiating instruction explores the reflection of the same material to all students using various instructional strategies. In addition, the teacher would explore delivering lessons at varying levels of difficulty based on each student's ability. Differentiated instruction is an approach to teaching where the teachers actively plan for students' differences so that they can explore learning in the best way possible. It is like "adapting content, process, or product" for teachers and administrators according to a specific student's "readiness, interest, and learning profile." This indeed leads to joyful learning in particular.

73. Expeditionary Learning

During Expeditionary Learning, the students learn by conducting "learning expeditions" rather than sitting in a classroom being taught one subject at a time. "Through the EL model, students are provided with an on-par learning environment both physically and with the curriculum that gives them the chance to explore something uncommon and creative. Expeditionary learning allows children to take education into their own hands. Expeditionary Learning primarily involves "Project-Based Learning." in totality.

74. Personalized Learning

PersonalizedPersonalised learning is an educational approach that aims to customise learning for each student's strengths, needs, skills and interests. Each student gets a learning plan based on what they know and how the learning is achieved at its best. The objective is to dwell on designing and structuring the learning to meet the needs of every student. It defines an educational approach that aims to cucustomiseearning for each student's strengths, needs, skills and interests. Each student gets a learning plan those on what he knows and how he learns best.

75. Game-Based Learning

As the name suggests, gaming or joyful engagement is the priority. The core concept behind game-based learning is teaching through repetition, failure and the accomplishment of goals. Video games are built on this principle. Fantasy elements characterise it, and it uses competitive exercises to motivate students to learn better. In addition, Game-based learning refers to borrowing certain gaming principles and applying them to real-life settings to engage users, particularly the students.

76. Conducting a Discussion

Discussion is a style that challenges students to be responsible for their education. Students are required to sit around a circle and are tasked to find new information together, which may include a talk, wait for answers, and ultimately think for themselves. An orderly format of discussion is also known as Brainstorming. This is an ideal way for various forums for the open-ended, collaborative exchange of ideas among a teacher and students towards furthering students thinking, learning, problem-solving, understanding, and innovation towards excellence.

77. Forums

The forums represent a community or a group for learning. It is defined as a space for discussing, creating and implementing innovative and creative learning methodologies and strategic partnerships between the students and the teacher within a classroom. It involves the process of group discussion and incorporates Class discussion. The objective is to have an interactive model by regularly asking open-ended questions. The teacher further observes and evaluates whether the students have contributed to progressing toward engagement.

78. Bulletin Boards

Bulletin boards are a powerful learning tool for preschool to high school and beyond classrooms. The Bulletin boards reflect a class or school's identity in a big way. It represents the school's mission, vision, and objective of the course or the session to be covered when used by the teacher. As a surface intended for posting public messages, it serves as a ready reckoner for the students.

79. Reading Assignments

The reading assignment is a format of teaching or evaluating a learning scenario where the teacher assigns the reading of a passage. The lesson is given a task assigned for individual study. These reading assessments and assignments help children assess what they understand about a text and even explore further learning.

80. Crossword Puzzles

Crossword Puzzles motivate students toward learning with joy and creativity. It encourages the students on the go and helps them extend their vocabulary knowledge. As a live example, forwarded through the News Papers and Magazines, the Language classes can well relate to finding words based on clues. Students can playfully learn new vocabulary in their native language or a foreign language. When teaching foreign languages, you could do the same and describe. Another fun way to use jigsaw puzzles in geography is to teach your students about vegetation in the unfamiliar words in the foreign language accordingly. The science teachers can use crosswords as well to teach terminology.

81. Jigsaw puzzle maps

These are the ancient educational tools intended to teach students to put together maps about their country or the world. Further in academics, the teachers use jigsaw puzzles in language lessons to let students practice their speaking skills. Teachers often introduce themselves by telling their names, hobbies, if they have kids or not, what they like or don't like and so on, etc. Try to switch things around with a jigsaw activity.

82. Mind Maps

A mind map is a learning tool that helps students create and share visual representations of things. For example, a chapter on Climate can depict a mind map accordingly. It describes what is taught during lectures, notes, and standard classroom procedures. In the conception of learning, a mind map is a diagram that visually links a central subject or concept to related concepts, ideas, words, items, or tasks. The implementation of Mind Maps in teaching has grown over time towards harnessing the creativity and execution towards excellence in the teaching and learning process. A mind mapping is done for what has been covered in the class to engage students, encourage creativity, and teach how to learn rather than simply memorising content.

These are integrated into emerging teaching techniques such as the Flipped Classroom and Design Thinking as a productive learning format with delight within classrooms.

83. Quality Circles

A QC or a Quality Circle is a group of 5 to 15 members, ideally, 8, who sit together in the form of a circle and brainstorm over issues related to real-life problems. They identify the causes of the pain and finally develop strategies to solve them. Finally, the methods are implemented for improvement. This process is a much talked about approach to gaining problem-solving skills and creativity on the go. A concept derived from Japan, it follows the culture of Kaizen, which means Change for the better. It can be for students as well as teachers.

84. PDCA Charts

Also known as Plan Do Check and Act (PDCA) Charts. It involves systematically testing possible solutions, assessing the results, and implementing the ones shown to work. The PDCA/PDSA cycle is a continuous loop of planning, doing, checking (or studying), and acting. The PDSA cycle is a systematic series of steps for gaining valuable learning and knowledge to improve a topic or process continuously. PDCA Charts provide a practical and straightforward approach to solving problems and managing change in a classroom situation.

85. DMAIC Approach

Define, Measure, Analyse, Inspect/ Improve and Control form a new way of understanding a topic or a situation. It is based on sustainable education development and the concepts of DMAIC (Define, Measure, Analyze, Improve, Control)-a six sigma process improvement methodology integrated as a quality strategy towards the improvement of process and learning.

The DMAIC template keeps students on track towards engaged classrooms and effective learning management. It focuses on identifying problems and using a systematic, scientific approach to problem-solving.

86. Flash Cards

Flashcards are a convenient resource to have and can be helpful at every class stage. They are a great way to present, practise and recycle vocabulary. When students become familiar with the activities used in class, they can be given out to early finishers to use in small groups.

Flashcards are not new to teaching and learning. Teachers have been using flashcards, flashcards, or flip cards to teach vocabulary and other concepts for a very long time. A new dimension based learning is also on the cards with the introduction of digital flashcards as a great learning tool.

87. Interviews

The interviewing process in a classroom scenario provides a unique method for evaluating what the students know and need to know.

It works on observatory evidence through interactions and is a modelled way to gain competency over a subject by the students and the teachers. It functions as an interactive communication and information sharing model among the students and teachers.

88. Surveys

It is one of the data capture formats for learning and exploring knowledge. A part of the experiential learning framework, it occupies the student's interests in a big way.

The Student surveys lead to essential learning and help improve teaching effectiveness via feedback. A student survey allows them to voice their common issues, needs, and desires. It also helps provide feedback on teachers' traits and improvement with the march of time.

89. Reading Aloud

A widespread primary and pre-primary teacher's activity of yesteryears is too familiar in schools. At times relate and refer to interesting paging of learning in higher grades.

From the student's point of view, it improves their information processing skills, vocabulary, and comprehension. The process, in a way, helps students become proficient readers and thinkers. Reading aloud is more than fun – it's an effective teaching strategy, and indeed, it facilitates teachers to expose students to exceptional literature.

90. Exhibition

An exhibition is a process to test the application of whatever has been taught or learned., The students, during this activity, learn and experience an opportunity, to apply the knowledge and information collected through various sources. Accordingly, the teacher acts as a facilitator and undergoes the chance to test the students on what and how much they have learned. We include projects, presentations, and products through which students "exhibit" what they have learned.

Technology plays a vital role here in showcasing the work in the audio, video and text combination as a demonstration of the work. This explores the learning objectives and the outcomes as expected. An exhibition is typically both a learning experience and an evaluation of academic progress and achievement for the students.

91. Exchange Programme

The exchange programme is a connection or networked learning over a passage of time. It is a study program in which students pursue education at one of the international institutions for six months to one year. We also have national and local schools where we share the learning environment.

Various models are being exhibited through technology via webinars and other digital platforms where the competency is shared and explored. An international exchange program can be an excellent way to broaden the experience and obtain valuable cultural insights with life skills contributing to building the overall personality.

92. Interactive Lecture

Interactive Lecture-based teaching is a format of instruction where the teachers act as facilitators and involve the students through regular interactions. They use technology and hands-on for demonstrations to encourage, motivate and engage the learners in the process. Here the teacher delivers a well-organized, tightly constructed, and highly polished presentation followed by an interactive Question and Answer session.

93. Film and Video

The Film and video include some fascinating ways to educate and entertain students about a particular concept. This way, the students are motivated towards understanding the picture the better as the understanding in process clubs it.

The understanding is evaluated by the end through discussions and interactions. This indicates a combo of the innovative format of visual education aids like video, online spectrum, live, online and even offline, which works a lot towards improving various skills in particular.

94. Design Thinking

Design Thinking or DT is a positive mindset approach toward learning through decision making as a priority. It aids in learning, collaboration, and problproblem-solving as a structured framework for identifying the causes of a problem as a challenge and helps gather information and generate potential solutions through Empathy, Ideation Prototype. It manipulates the spectrum of Design Thinking in Education through the attribution of Empathy, Challenge, Discovery, and Sharing.

95. Personalised Instruction

It is one of the primary forms of learning and teaching. It refers to instruction-based education in which the pace of knowledge and the instructional approach are optimised for the needs of each learner.

As a Learner Centric and Specific learning format, it fascinates learning towards priority. Learning objectives, instructional approaches, and content (and sequencing) may vary based on learner needs.

96. Recitation

A recitation, in a general sense,e is the act of reciting from memory or a formal reading of a verse or other writing before an audience.

The definition of a recitation is the telling of details, or the act of saying something that's been memorised out loud, or the thing that is read.

97. Memorization

It defines the means of learning by self. Many students feel like they do not have strong memory skills. Fortunately, though, memorising is not just for an elite group of people born with the right skills—anyone can train and develop their memorising abilities.

98. Reasoning

This concerns the critical way of learning and exploring the new unknown. Logical reasoning determines if algorithms will work by predicting what happens when the algorithm's steps - and the rules they consist of - are followed. Predictions from each algorithm can be used to compare solutions and decide on the best one.

99. Social-Emotional Learning

Social-emotional learning (SEL) develops self-awareness, self-control, and interpersonal skills necessary for school, work, and life success. People with strong social-emotional skills better cope with daily life challenges and benefit academically, professionally, and socially.

This strategy occupies an emotional connection with the teachers among the students. Targeting the development of these skills can translate into higher academic achievement, among other gains. It includes management skills, among others. It creates an environment conducive to learning and is promoted through explicit instruction to the students.

100. Instructional scaffolding

Instructional scaffolding is a process through which a teacher supports students to enhance learning and assist in the mastery of tasks. Here, the instructor systematically builds on students' experiences and knowledge while learning the new skills.

About The Author

Dheeraj Mehrotra, MS, MPhil, PhD (Education Management) honoris causa., a white and a yellow belt in SIX SIGMA, a Certified NLP Business Diploma holder, is an Educational Innovator, Author, with expertise in Six Sigma In Education, Academic Audits, Neuro-Linguistic Programming (NLP), Total Quality Management In Education, an Experiential Educator, a CBSE Resource towards School Assessment (SQAA), CCE, JIT, Five S, and KAIZEN. He has authored over 40 books on Computer Science for ICSE/ ISC/ CBSE Students, over 60 books of academic interest for the field of education excellence, and Six Sigma. A former Principal at De Indian Public School, New Delhi, (INDIA) with an ample teaching experience of over Two Decades, he is a certified Trainer for Quality Circles/ TQM in Education and QCI Standards for School

Accreditation/ Six Sigma in Education. He has also been honoured with the President of India's National Teacher Award in the year 2006 and the Best Science Teacher State Award (By the Ministry of Science and Technology, State of UP), Innovation in Education for his inception of Six Sigma In Education by Education Watch, New Delhi and Education World- Best Teacher Award, BOLT Learner Teacher Award by Air India, 'Innovation in Education Award 2016' by Higher Education Forum (HEF), Gujarat Chapter, among others. He has developed over 150 FREE EDUCATIONAL MOBILE Apps for the Google Play Store exclusively for Teachers, Students, and Parents. This work has been recognised by the LIMCA BOOK OF RECORDS & INDIA BOOK OF RECORDS as the only Indian to draw that feast. Dr Mehrotra is presently working as a PRINCIPAL at KUNWARS GLOBAL SCHOOL and Lucknow in India. He has conducted over 1000 workshops globally on "Excellence In Education" integrated with Total Quality Management and Six Sigma, Technology Integration in Education (TIE), Developing towards being ROCKSTAR TEACHERS, including Cyberspace, Cyber Security, Classroom Management, School Leadership & Management, and Innovative teaching within classrooms via Mind Maps, NLP and Experiential Learning in Academics. He is an active TEDx speaker and can be viewed on the youtube TEDx channel. As a premium UDEMY Instructor, he has also developed over 450 courses and is catering to over 8 Lakh students from 180 plus countries. He can be visited at www.authordheerajmehrotra.com.

Some Books By The Same Author

SOME BOOKS BY THE SAME AUTHOR

Enter Caption

Printed by Libri Plureos GmbH in Hamburg,
Germany